NATIVE ❖ LATIN ❖ AMERICAN ❖ CULTURES

EUROPEAN CONQUEST

Eileen Lucas

Series Editor:
Robert Pickering, Ph.D.

❖   ❖   ❖

ROURKE PUBLICATIONS, INC.
Vero Beach, Florida 32964

Printed in the United States of America.

A Blackbirch Graphics book.

Senior Editor: Tanya Lee Stone
Assistant Editor: Elizabeth Taylor
Design Director: Sonja Kalter

Library of Congress Cataloging-in-Publication Data

Lucas, Eileen.
European conquest / by Eileen Lucas.
    p. cm. — (Native Latin American cultures)
    Includes index.
    ISBN 0-86625-556-7
    1. Indians—First contact with Europeans—Juvenile literature. 2. Indians of Mexico—History—Juvenile literature. 3. Indians of South America—History—Juvenile literature. 4. Mexico—History—Conquest, 1519–1540—Juvenile literature. 5. Peru—History—Conquest, 1522–1548—Juvenile literature. 6. America—Discovery and exploration—Spanish—Juvenile literature. [1. Indians—First contact with Europeans. 2. America—Discovery and exploration—Spanish.] I. Title. II. Series.
E59.F53L83   1996
970.01—dc20   95-5426
                                                                         CIP
                                                                          AC

Contents

Introduction

The towering temples and fierce warriors of the Aztecs, the sophisticated lords of the Maya, and the vast empire of the Inca that extended along the Andes are all images that come to mind when the native cultures of Mexico, Central America, and South America are mentioned. While these images are real, they are only a small part of the story of the indigenous peoples of the Americas. More important, there are hundreds of other cultures that are not as well known, but just as interesting. To explore the cultures of this huge area is to examine the great diversity and richness of humanity in the Americas.

This series on *Native Latin American Cultures* presents six books, each with a major theme: the arts, daily customs, spirituality, trade, tribal rules, and the invasion by Europeans. It focuses mainly on pre-Columbian times (before the arrival of Columbus in the New World) through about 1800. These books illustrate the ingenuity, resourcefulness, and unique characters of many cultures. While a variety of tribes share similarities, many are extremely different from one another.

It is important to remember that the Americas were home to people long before Europeans arrived. Archaeologists have uncovered sites as old as 12,000 years. Over the years, human cultures in every part of the Americas developed and evolved. Some native cultures died out, other peoples survived as hunter-gatherers, and still others grew to

❖

5

create huge empires. Many native languages were not recorded and, in some instances, they have been forgotten.

But other groups, such as the Maya, did record their languages. Scientists are just now learning to read the Mayan language. Mayan stories tell of the power and glory of great rulers, heroic battles between city-states, and other important events. Massive stone temples and ruins of cities have survived from several cultures, giving us insight into the past.

Many native cultures of the Americas exist today. Some have blended with the modern cultures of their countries while maintaining their traditional ways. Other, more remote groups exist much as they did several hundred years ago. The books in the *Native Latin American Cultures* series capture the richness of indigenous cultures of the Americas, bringing past cultures alive and exploring those that have survived.

Robert Pickering, Ph.D.
Department of Anthropology
Denver Museum of Natural History

Chapter

1

The Caribbean Islands and the Caribbean Coast of South America

Scientists believe that the first "invasion" of the Americas took place about 30,000 years ago, when nomads crossed the Bering Strait from Asia into North America. Over thousands of years, these peoples and their descendants spread out across the Americas.

Life must have been very difficult for these ancient peoples, as they searched for food and suitable places to live. They survived by learning what plants were edible, and by hunting animals with weapons made of stone and wood. Slowly, they moved to all corners of the North and South American continents. Archaeologists estimate that there were people in Central and South America by 9000 B.C., and possibly even earlier.

Over time, these wandering hunters broke up into separate groups of people and developed distinctive cultures. By 1500 B.C., many of them were farming such plants as

7

corn, or maize, in the dryer climates, and manioc, or cassava, in the more humid regions. In some places, they settled structured villages. Over time, some groups, such as the Toltecs, Maya, Aztecs, and Inca, developed complex cultures and built large, impressive cities. Others, such as the Caribs, Arawaks, Chichimecs, and Tupi, continued to move from place to place, relying on hunting and gathering of wild foods to survive.

Some lived in thick jungles and had little contact with other groups. Many of the native groups in Mexico, Central America, and South America, however, participated in extensive trading networks. In this way, they shared products and ideas with each other.

Life was full of challenges for these peoples. Sometimes there were wars between tribes, and more powerful groups conquered and controlled their weaker neighbors. Religious leaders helped tribal peoples to understand the world around them. None of the things they had developed—their farms, cities, trading networks, and religions—could help them predict what would happen in the future. None of them could know how their lives would change forever when large white sails appeared on the horizon to the east.

The Arrival of Columbus

On October 12, 1492, three ships that had sailed across the Atlantic Ocean from Spain landed on the shores of a beautiful island. The Taino people who lived there called the island Guanahani. The captain of the sailing ships, Christopher Columbus, called it San Salvador. He wanted to believe that he had arrived at an island off the coast of Asia, for he was in search of the gold and spices of the Indies.

Believing that he had landed in the Indies, Columbus called the people he met Indians. They were friendly, and so willing to imitate the Spaniards as they made the sign of the cross, that Columbus thought they would make fine Christians. Because they tried to please the Spanish visitors in many other ways as well, Columbus also believed that they would make fine servants.

For a while, the Spanish called any native people who they met Indians. It took some time for them to observe that the various groups of people were different in many ways and that they belonged, in fact, to many different tribes.

The gentle, friendly inhabitants of San Salvador, the Taino, were of the Arawak family of tribes. The Arawaks had spread throughout the Caribbean region and the Amazon Basin and were found as far south as Argentina. They had broken into many tribal groups, but they spoke a common language and had similar customs. Their primary enemy, before the arrival of the Spanish, was the Carib tribe.

The Carib culture was different from that of the Taino and other Arawak tribes. They were bold adventurers who struck terror in the hearts of their enemies. To be captured by the Caribs meant torture and death. Sometimes, it also meant being cannibalized. That is, under certain circumstances, the Caribs ate the bodies of their enemies after killing them. This was usually done as part of a religious ceremony.

Although some other native groups in this part of the world practiced cannibalism, those that the Spanish first became aware of were the Caribs, and their name became synonymous with cannibalism. The Spanish, however, started to call any of the native people they did not like Caribs. This was because in 1503, Queen Isabella of Spain had decreed that since the Caribs were not Christians, it was acceptable to make them slaves. Thus, any time the Spanish wanted to make slaves of—or were having trouble with—native peoples, they labeled them Caribs. This allowed the

After Columbus returned to Spain, it is believed that the Spanish settlers that he left behind at Navidad were massacred by members of a native tribe.

Spanish to enslave, and sometimes kill, the Caribs with the queen's blessing. After all, she was thousands of miles away, and checking on her adventurers was a difficult task.

Europeans of the time believed that unless a land was already owned by another European nation, it was "free" to be claimed for their own. The fact that people were already living in the Americas did not impress Columbus. He claimed the island of San Salvador (and its people) for Spain, and then traveled to a nearby island, which he named Hispaniola (the site of the present-day nations of Haiti and the Dominican Republic). There he left some of his crew behind in a settlement called Navidad, while he returned to Spain with a few of the Arawaks he had captured and a small amount of gold. When he returned on a second voyage, the

Spaniards who had remained at Navidad were all dead. Some tribes reported that the men had been killed by other tribes the Spaniards had mistreated.

Perhaps it was at this point that the Spanish began to notice that the people they called Indians were not all the same. It is likely that there were both Carib and Arawak tribes living on Hispaniola when Christopher Columbus first landed there. This, however, seems not to have mattered much to the Spanish soldiers, most of whom were willing to mistreat all the natives equally.

Columbus was disappointed that he was finding very little gold and lots of natives, so he decided to send some of the natives to Spain to be sold as slaves. On his return to the islands, Columbus sent 500 natives to Spain. Nearly half of them died at sea, and many others died soon after landing in Europe.

Queen Isabella not only financed Columbus's voyage to the New World, but also encouraged the enslavement of the native peoples he encountered in the Caribbean.

Things were not much better for the tribal groups that remained behind. The Spanish soldiers who had come with Columbus built a permanent settlement on Hispaniola, but they did not make good colonists. They terrorized and abused the natives and got angry when Columbus, who had been appointed governor of the islands by Queen Isabella and King Ferdinand, tried to punish them as well as the natives. The soldiers complained about Columbus to the king and queen, and he was removed as governor.

Yet even with a new governor, conditions did not improve for the native peoples of the islands. Thousands

In the 1500s, Bartolomé de Las Casas championed the rights of native peoples living in Spanish settlements in the Caribbean. He helped get laws passed to protect natives from Spanish cruelties.

of them were forced to work for the Spanish, mostly panning gold from the rivers. When they had no gold to give to the Spaniards, they were beaten or killed. If any of them tried to escape into the mountains, they were hunted down with dogs.

To make matters worse, the native peoples of the Americas had no immunity to such European diseases as smallpox and influenza. After being weakened by abusive treatment, many of the natives were vulnerable to these diseases. Within half a century of the arrival of the Europeans, many of the natives of the islands were dead.

In contrast, there were a few Spaniards who tried to help the natives. Among the greatest of these was a colonist who later became a Dominican priest. His name was Bartolomé de Las Casas. Beginning in 1514, he gave up his own land and began to fight against the enslavement of the natives. Thanks to his efforts, laws were passed in Spain to protect the natives in the colonies. Unfortunately, these laws were seldom enforced, and even when they were, it was too late to stop the decimation of the peoples of the Caribbean.

As the natives continued to die, African people were brought to the islands to replace them as slaves. In time, they would become the main inhabitants of the islands, and the Taino and others would become extinct.

Other Europeans Before Columbus

It is likely that other Europeans set foot in various places on the shores of the Americas before Columbus did. Saint Brendan, an Irish monk, is believed by some to have been one of the earliest visitors to the New World. According to legend, he and other Irish monks crossed the Atlantic in small, round, tublike boats around A.D. 500.

Many historians also believe that some Viking explorers visited the northeastern coast of North America around A.D. 1000. They established one or more settlements in a land they called Vinland, somewhere between Newfoundland and Massachusetts. If this is accurate, these explorers probably would have interacted with a number of North American native groups. Whatever settlements they may have established, however, were abandoned well before Columbus arrived in the Caribbean.

Some scientists also think that America may have been visited in early times by people who traveled across the Pacific Ocean from either Asia or the islands of Polynesia.

So, if Columbus was not the first European to reach the Americas, were his voyages still important? Yes, say historians. Within fifty years of his landing in the Caribbean, there were Europeans exploring, conquering, and establishing settlements across South America, from the mouth of the Amazon River to the Andes mountains, along the Caribbean coast from Venezuela to Florida, and up the Atlantic coast of North America to the Saint Lawrence Seaway. European kingdoms waged wars over the control of the oceans between the continents and for the colonies in the new lands. It was the arrival of the *Niña*, the *Pinta*, and the *Santa María* that marked the beginning of this full-scale invasion of the New World by the Old World.

On to the Mainland

On Columbus's third voyage, in 1498, he spied the coast of the continent of South America from the island of Trinidad. He landed there briefly, but as he knew that it could not be China, he did not explore this great landmass.

Other explorers, however, did. Amerigo Vespucci sailed along the Atlantic and Caribbean coasts of the continent and noticed different groups of native peoples. He described these peoples of the New World, as he called it, in dramatic letters that gained him much fame. Soon this land was being named "America," in his honor, on some maps.

In 1499, a Spaniard named Alonso de Ojeda explored the warm-water shores of the northern coast of South America. There he came upon natives gathering pearls, which he purchased with trinkets. In the Gulf of Maracaibo he saw a native village built over the water on stilts. He called it Venezuela, or "Little Venice," which became the name of that South American country. Many of the people of this region were of the fierce Carib family of tribes, or of the distantly related Arawak family.

A number of tribes also lived along the Caribbean coast of Colombia. One of these was the Guajiro, who were hunter-gatherers. When the Spanish introduced domestic animals, such as cattle, sheep, and goats to this area, the Guajiro adopted them for their use as well.

In 1502, Columbus returned to the Caribbean for his fourth and last time. He was still looking for a way to get past the islands and on to the Far East. He sailed along the coast of Central America, from Honduras to Panama, not knowing that the Pacific Ocean was just over the mountains.

Among the native groups that he observed were the San Blas people, who lived primarily on the coral islands off Panama. Largely because Columbus and later explorers passed them by, the San Blas and other members of the

Cuna tribe are still found in this area, living much as they did 500 years ago.

On April 16, 1503, 12 Spaniards were killed by a force of 400 natives at a garrison the Spanish had built north of Panama. This was one of the first significant attacks on the Spaniards by the native people, who were beginning to tire of the Spaniards' dominating ways.

After surviving the attack and escaping from Panama, Columbus was shipwrecked on the island of Jamaica and marooned there for a year. Without the aid of the natives, who gave him and his crew food, and who sold one of his men a canoe with which to paddle to Hispaniola for help, Columbus and his crew would have perished.

Meanwhile, other Spaniards were sailing across the Atlantic on expeditions. The islands of Hispaniola and Cuba served for some time as the Spanish base of operations. As the forests of these islands were leveled and the gold was exhausted, however, new settlement sites became necessary. Forts and trading posts were established along the Caribbean coast of Central and South America.

From one of these posts, a conquistador, or conqueror, named Vasco Núñez de Balboa set out to find the great body of water—"always calm and pacific"—that the natives had told him about. Unlike many of the other conquistadores, Balboa got along well with many of the local tribes.

In 1513, Balboa succeeded in crossing the isthmus (a narrow strip of land), and claimed the waters of the Pacific Ocean for Spain. The Spanish would sail both north and south from this western shore of Central America in their continuing quest for gold.

A statue of Vasco Núñez de Balboa stands in Panama City, Panama. Balboa began his search for the Pacific Ocean from the Isthmus of Panama.

The Central Valley of Mexico

From the islands of the Caribbean, the Spanish ventured into what is now Mexico. Landing first along the northern edge of the Yucatán Peninsula, they encountered groups of natives called Maya. When they asked these people where they would find gold, the people pointed to the northwest and replied, "Mejico, Mejico."

The Conquistador Cortés

When the Spaniards came ashore farther up the coast, they found native peoples who paid tribute, or tax, to a more powerful group in the interior. In 1519, led by Hernando Cortés, they occupied the town of Tabasco and defeated the local tribes. Cortés accepted the natives' gifts and asked for their help in conquering the great kingdom of the interior, that of the Aztecs. He was able to communicate with the people of Mexico because he had several interpreters who could speak both Spanish and native languages. One of these was a Spaniard who had been shipwrecked earlier along the Yucatán coast and had served as a slave to the

Opposite:
Before reaching the Aztec capital of Tenochtitlán, Hernando Cortés fought with smaller tribes. Here, Cortés meets strong opposition from a tribe in the Tlascan territory.

17

Maya. The other was a native woman the Spaniards named Doña Marina who could speak the languages of both the Aztecs and the Maya. Because Cortés could communicate with the natives through these interpreters, he was able to take advantage of weaknesses in their political-alliance system. That is, he was able to make friends with the Aztecs' enemies. The enemies, however, mistakenly thought it was they who were taking advantage of Cortés.

Cortés's plan was to enlist the aid of independent native groups to help him fight the Aztecs as he moved toward the interior plateau where they lived. After heavy fighting, he defeated a native group called the Tlaxcalans, who hated and feared the Aztec emperor Moctezuma. They then agreed to become Cortés's allies.

Next, Cortés fought with and conquered a tribe called the Cholulans, large numbers of whom were killed by the superior Spanish weaponry. The survivors joined his forces. These native allies would later be very important to Cortés's defeat of the Aztecs. Without them, it would have been virtually impossible for just 500 Spaniards to vanquish the thousands of warriors who served Moctezuma.

Cortés's next stop was the Aztec capital, Tenochtitlán. This great city was one of the largest in the world at that time, and one of many city-states in the valley of Mexico. There were both alliance and competition among these powerful city-states. Tenochtitlán was built on a lake and could be entered only by crossing over one of several bridges, called causeways, with removable sections. The Aztecs had ruled from this spot until the arrival of the Spanish.

Moctezuma knew that Cortés was approaching and waited for him inside his palace, trying to decide what to do. Aztec legend said that Quetzalcoatl, the plumed serpent god, would one day return from the sea. Moctezuma thought that perhaps this invader was he.

In this engraving, Cortés and his army conquer the Cholulans.

Moctezuma, however, had also heard things that made him suspect Cortés was simply a human aggressor. He sent messengers to Cortés, offering to give him a great deal of treasure if he would leave Mexico forever. This, however, just convinced Cortés that the Aztec capital would be a great prize, and he marched onward.

As Cortés, with his Spanish soldiers and native allies, advanced into Tenochtitlán, Moctezuma came out to greet them. Researchers believe that his plan was to be friendly to the invaders until he could think of a way to get rid of them. Moctezuma led them to his guest quarters and gave the Spaniards gifts. The Spaniards were amazed at the size and beauty of Tenochtitlán. The temples and shrines were decorated with beautiful ornaments and figures made of precious metals. The Spaniards compared it to Venice, one of the finest, cleanest cities in all of Europe.

The Spanish, however, refused to act as guests. They took Moctezuma prisoner and held him hostage in his own city. They knew that the Aztec people were very unhappy about the presence of the Spanish, and the Spanish hoped to keep the Aztecs under control by keeping their king prisoner.

Several months later, while Cortés was out of the city, some of his soldiers attacked and killed hundreds of Aztecs during one of their religious festivals. Cortés hurried back to the city, with Spanish reinforcements, but things had already gotten out of hand in Tenochtitlán. He feared that the Aztec people would kill them all. He asked Moctezuma to talk to his people, but the emperor was hit in the head with a rock during the fighting and died soon afterward.

One night, hoping that most of the Aztec warriors would be asleep, Cortés ordered a retreat from the city. The Aztecs were waiting for them, and a bloody battle over the causeways followed. Several hundred Spaniards and perhaps as many as 4,000 Aztecs died in the hand-to-hand combat. The Spaniards named this *Noche Triste*, Night of Sorrow. It took them six days to reach the safety of the coast, with heavy fighting all the way. The Spaniards were slowed in their retreat from the city because they were loaded up with stolen treasure.

Tenochtitlán is re-created in a mural. Spanish invaders were amazed by the city's beauty and size.

The Conquest of Tenochtitlán

In Tlaxcala, Cortés and his men nursed their wounds, acquired reinforcements, and planned another attack. In Tenochtitlán, the Aztecs, under their new emperor Cuauhtemoc, a leader of great courage, sacrificed the prisoners they had taken and prepared to defend their city against the onslaught they knew would be coming.

As the many tribes forced to become part of the Aztec empire saw it being weakened by the Spanish, they stopped paying tribute, including food, to Tenochtitlán. This added to the hardships of the Aztecs in the capital city.

Moreover, the Spaniards had been in Mexico long enough to spread the diseases that would be so deadly to the native people. A smallpox epidemic raged across the Mexican countryside, and according to some estimates, wiped out about a third of the native population.

On December 29, 1520, Cortés left Tlaxcala and headed to Tenochtitlán. Besides about 550 Spaniards, he commanded approximately 10,000 native allies. However, there were at least that number, and probably many more, Aztec warriors waiting for them in the city on the lake. Cortés began his siege of the city on April 28, 1521.

First, he destroyed the aqueduct that brought fresh water into the city. Then, he took control of the bridges, which prevented the Aztecs inside the city from leaving and from receiving supplies. He even had boats built with which to attack the city from the water.

As Cortés and his men entered Tenochtitlán, they destroyed every building they could, to keep the Aztecs from attacking from the rooftops. Cortés repeatedly asked the Aztecs to surrender. Again and again came the brave reply that the Aztecs would fight to the last man.

For three months, the fighting went on. Finally, Moctezuma's heir, Cuauhtemoc, was captured, and the

In a mural by Mexican artist Diego Rivera, the deadly battle between the Spanish and the Aztecs is depicted. Here, Cortés (center) attacks the Aztec Sun Warrior.

battle came to an end. On August 13, 1521, Tenochtitlán and, thus, the Aztec empire, fell to the Spanish. When Cuauhtemoc was asked why he had kept fighting when it was inevitable that Cortés would win, he is supposed to have said, "I have defended my city, my kingdom, just as he would have defended his had I attempted to take it away from him."

From then on, the Aztec empire was ruled by representatives of the Spanish court. The native people who had

❖

23

paid tribute to the Aztecs in the past now had to pay even more to the Spanish. The Aztecs themselves were forced to work on the great Spanish plantations and in the gold and silver mines. They were also forced to accept the Spanish way of life. Never again would they worship their gods from the great pyramid temples that they had built, or receive great riches in tribute from all the tribes of the region. Their imperial state had been replaced by another one, harsher and foreign.

In just three years (1519–1521), Cortés had destroyed a great civilization that had been built up over many generations. Almost immediately, however, a new city was built on the ruins of Tenochtitlán. It was called Mexico City, and soon it was a very central part of the Spanish empire in the Americas.

From the children who would be born of Spanish fathers and native mothers, a new culture would be born. An inscription on a temple in Mexico City says of the fall of Tenochtitlán, "This was neither a victory nor a defeat. It was the anguished birth of the mestizo nation that is the Mexico of today."

After the conquest of Tenochtitlán, the mestizo, or mixed-blood, population of Mexico rapidly increased. Soon the majority of people were of both Spanish and Mexican ancestry. There were areas of central Mexico, however, in which people of pure native ancestry remained. People tried to live as close to the old ways of the Aztecs as possible but, more often, blended the Spanish ways with their traditional culture. One young man, Benito Juárez, eventually became the president of Mexico, a title that did not exist in the days of Tenochtitlán. Nahuatl, the language of the Aztecs, is the third most widely spoken native language in the Americas today, just after the South American native languages of Quechua and Guaraní.

Northwestern Mexico

After Cortés destroyed the Aztec empire and Mexico City became the capital of the Spanish empire in the Americas, the Spanish set out on expeditions farther northward into Mexico. Cortés also ordered explorations by sea along the western shores of Mexico, as far north as California.

Early Explorers

Some explorers entered Mexico from the northeast. One of these was Álvar Núñez Cabeza de Vaca, who walked across Texas and Mexico after being shipwrecked near Galveston, Texas, in 1528. He and the three men with him (two Spanish soldiers and an African man named Esteban) gained a reputation as healers, and made friends with the many tribes whose territories they passed through. When Cabeza de Vaca finally met up with Spanish forces in northwestern Mexico in 1536, he was angered by the arrogance of the

Opposite:
In Chihuahua,
Batopilas Canyon
rises above La Bufa.
During the 1500s,
explorers encountered
landscape such as this
in northern Mexico.

Álvar Núñez Cabeza de Vaca befriended many native tribes as he walked across Mexico and Texas.

Spanish soldiers, who wanted to enslave the natives who had come with him as friends and guides.

Other explorers came up across the mountains and deserts from Mexico City. Among these were two Spaniards named Guzmán. One was Nuño de Guzmán. In the 1550s, he began to push the frontier northward, from the area known as Sinaloa, in the west, toward what is now the Mexican state of Sonora. Along the rivers of this otherwise very dry and rugged region, Guzmán found clusters of native villages.

One of his captains was a man named Diego de Guzmán. As he explored the territory that now comprises the Mexican states of Durango, Chihuahua, and Sonora, he encountered several groups of native people. These included the Mayo, Yaqui, Pima, and Opata tribes, farmers who raised such food crops as corn, beans, and squash. They enjoyed settled lives in small villages. These natives were the same people who had befriended Cabeza de Vaca.

In contrast, the Seri, another group of people of the Sonora region explored by Diego de Guzmán, were hunter-gatherers. They lived a seminomadic life, which means that they moved about within their territory in search of food. Through their brutality and abuse, the Guzmáns nearly depopulated this region. Their terrible excesses disturbed and offended even the Spaniards.

The Coronado Expedition

Another Spanish explorer was Francisco Vásquez de Coronado. In 1540, he left Mexico City at the head of a force of Spanish soldiers, native allies, and Franciscan priests. They also had an assortment of livestock to be used for food along the way. They set out to convert natives to Christianity. They were also searching for the legendary Seven Cities of Cibola, supposedly filled with unimaginable treasures. The farther Coronado pushed into Mexico and beyond into present-day Arizona, New Mexico, Texas, and Oklahoma, the more he realized that the fabled cities were just that—

A door panel on the Iglesia de San Francisco in Sante Fe, New Mexico, shows a Spanish priest seeing a Zuni pueblo for the first time in 1539.

fables. What he found was pueblo villages, with multistory homes built of clay. Perhaps these villages had glittered in the hot desert sun and looked like cities of gold to someone at a distance.

Though the pueblo villages did not contain gold, they did have something the Spaniards desperately needed. Without the food stored in the pueblo villages of what are now Arizona and New Mexico, Coronado and his men would have starved to death. The fact that the natives would go hungry after the soldiers ate all their food did not stop the Spanish. They even attacked, without provocation, what had been a friendly Zuni village, letting the natives know that they were conquerors, not friends.

From the Zuni villages, Coronado sent out exploring parties in several directions. One of these headed southwest along the Gulf of California coast of Mexico. The expedition's leader, Melchior Díaz, crossed what to him seemed a lifeless desert. He called it El Camino del Diablo—"The Devil's Road."

When Coronado eventually returned to northern Mexico with all of his troops, he discovered that the base camps he had left behind had been destroyed by tribes who had objected to how they had been treated by the Spaniards. Coronado hurriedly left and returned to the safety of Mexico City, where he was reprimanded and some of his officers punished for mistreating the natives.

The Missions

After Coronado's discouraging reports, few Spaniards ventured into the northwestern part of Mexico for years. From time to time, a few Jesuit missionaries would try to convert various native groups to Christianity, but they had little effect on the people, and some were even killed.

The Jesuits, however, were determined in their work, and missions gradually began to appear. The goal of the missionaries was to bring Catholicism, as well as the Spanish culture and economic system, to the tribes with the help of native labor. They put up buildings and created farms. Because many of the local tribes had already been successful farmers and lived in permanent villages, they adapted easily to the mission way of life. The loyalty of such native groups as the Pima and the Opata enabled the Jesuits to slowly expand their missions northward into California. The Seri, however, were used to living independently and they generally resisted the efforts of the missionaries and others to "civilize" them.

In some parts of northwestern Mexico, missionaries were followed by miners and other settlers. As the number of Spanish and mestizo people in the region increased, so did the inevitable outbreaks of disease. In 1615, some of the Seri fled southward toward Mexico City, hoping to escape an epidemic of bubonic plague, which was killing many of them. They had no way of knowing that the plague had actually originated in Mexico City and that many of them would die when they got there.

There were many other outbreaks of diseases that the natives could not fight, such as scarlet fever in 1637, and smallpox in 1639. These epidemics greatly reduced the population of native people in northwestern Mexico.

The missionaries did whatever they could to help the natives, giving them what medicine they had available. In the 1680s, for example, Father Eurebio Francisco Kino was one of those who worked tirelessly among the Pima tribe and other groups of the Sonora region.

Over the next few centuries, however, uprisings among the native peoples would occur as they tried to regain their land and their way of life. These rebellions invariably ended with the deaths of natives and more hardship. Some of the tribes resigned themselves to the presence of the Spanish, and some even seemed to welcome them. The Pima, in particular, were helpful to miners who traveled through their territory in search of precious minerals, and, along with the Opata, they cooperated with the U.S. government in its war with the Apache people to the north. Many of the descendants of the natives of northwestern Mexico have been assimilated into the mestizo culture. However, there remain small bands of native groups in this region today who maintain many of their old traditions.

In New Mexico, ruins of the Pecos Mission church still stand today. Spanish missionaries established churches and farms to assist them in bringing Christianity and Spanish culture to native tribes in northern Mexico.

Chapter

Southern Mexico, Yucatán, and Central America

In the southernmost part of Mexico, in the Yucatán Peninsula, and in the northern portion of Central America, lived a group of people called the Maya. From the time around 2500 B.C. to the arrival of the Spanish, their culture went through both periods of greatness and times of civil war. Between the years A.D. 250 and 900, known as the Classic Period of Mayan civilization, they built large cities with pyramids, palaces, and roads. These were mostly in the highlands of what are now Guatemala and Honduras. For an unknown reason, the Maya abandoned these cities and most of them moved northward into the Yucatán Peninsula. There they built new cities and were influenced by a group of Toltecs who had moved down from the central valley of Mexico.

In 1441, Mayapan, one of the most important cities of the Mayan region, was destroyed during civil warfare. One group, the Itzá Maya, fled to Lake Petén Itzá, deep within the jungles of southern Yucatán. The rest of the Maya lived in small, independent city-states scattered throughout their territory. Each city had its own government, and there was little cooperation among them. There was no capital, and no central figure of authority.

First Contacts

The first contact between the Maya and the Europeans occurred in 1502, when Christopher Columbus sailed down the coast of Honduras on his fourth voyage to the "Indies." One day, the explorer's ship was approached by a large canoe filled with Maya on a trading mission to the island of Cozumel. The Maya visited briefly aboard what must have seemed to them a huge ship. They exchanged a few trade items with the Spaniards. Columbus learned that these people were of a culture very different from that of the natives of the Caribbean islands. He sailed on. The Maya returned to their villages and described what they saw: large ships, like houses, floating on the water and pale-skinned, bearded sailors whose chief had the pale skin, red hair, and blue eyes of Quetzalcoatl, the plumed serpent god.

Over the next few years, the Maya would hear of additional sightings of the large ships and bearded strangers. In 1511, a small group of Spaniards, whose ship had sunk off the coast of Jamaica, was washed ashore in the Yucatán. The leader and a few of the soldiers were sacrificed by the Mayan cacique, or chief, who had captured them, but several were allowed to live.

Two of the people who survived later escaped. One man, Gonzalo de Guerrero, would serve the Maya as a slave until the arrival of Cortés. At that time, he was allowed to

In Diego Rivera's mural "The Legend of Quetzalcoatl" the plumed serpent god is represented by a fair-skinned, bearded man. The Maya, as well as other native peoples of the area, believed some of the Spanish invaders were the embodiment of Quetzalcoatl.

leave, and he became one of the interpreters who helped Cortés communicate with the natives of Mexico. The other was Geronimo de Aguilar. He married a Mayan woman and became a great warrior for the Maya, eventually dying in a battle against the invading Spanish.

In 1517, a battle took place between the Maya along the Yucatán coast and the Spanish. Led by Francisco Hernandez de Cordoba, the Spaniards landed near Cape Catoche, the site of an established Mayan town. It was one of the first with streets, pyramids, and houses built of stone that the Spaniards had seen in the New World.

The Mayan villagers had been friendly at first, but when the Spaniards began to help themselves to the water supply, the natives attacked. Fresh water was a precious commodity in this area and the Maya would not allow the Spaniards to use it all for themselves. The Spanish were sent running for their ships under a shower of arrows.

The same thing happened when they landed a little farther up the coast, at a place called Champotón. Fifty Spaniards were killed there and Cordoba himself was wounded at least ten times. He later died of his battle injuries.

Those who did survive brought home tales of gold. The next year, another party of Spaniards, this time led by Juan de Grijalva, landed at Champotón. Mayan warriors armed with bows and arrows waited for them on the shore. The Spaniards fired their guns into the ranks of the warriors, driving them off the beach. After staying at Champotón for a few days, the Spaniards sailed on, searching for treasure.

Hoping to avoid warfare with the Spanish, the Maya permitted Hernando Cortés to travel through their lands in 1524.

As they traded with the Maya, they heard stories of riches to the north, in "Mejico," and it was there that the Spanish would focus their attention for the next few years.

When the Maya learned that the Spaniard Cortés had landed in Mexico and had attacked the Aztecs, they hoped that this meant that they would be left alone. For a short time they were.

In 1524, the Maya allowed Cortés to pass through their territory on his way to Honduras to fight a fellow Spaniard who had become too independent. In fact, many of the Mayan villages that Cortés passed through were deserted. At this point, it seems, many of the Maya thought that keeping as much distance as possible between themselves and the Spanish soldiers was the best policy.

Cuauhtemoc, the last emperor of the Aztecs, was still Cortés's prisoner at this time and had been brought along on this journey. When the Aztec leader was accused of trying to talk Cortés's native allies into killing him, the Spaniard had him killed.

War in the Yucatán

In 1527, the Spanish again came to Mayan territory to make war on the Maya. In a number of battles in the Yucatán, hundreds of Maya were killed. At the same time, other Spanish forces were fighting the Maya to the south, in what is now Guatemala.

Over the next few years, various Spanish expeditions would travel through Mayan lands. Sometimes, they met with hostility and would have to fight; at other times, the Maya offered little physical resistance in the face of the Spaniards' superior weapons.

The Spanish found that conquering the Maya would be very different from how conquering the Aztecs had been. It would take much longer and would have to be

❖

36

accomplished city by city, since there was no unified empire that would fall on the death of one leader or the destruction of one city. With their advanced weaponry and constant reinforcements, however, the Spaniards began to gain control of Mayan territory.

In 1542, the Spaniards occupied Tiho, near the great Mayan city of Chichén Itzá. They named it Mérida, today the capital of Yucatán. They told the Maya that their customs were bad and that the Spanish ways were good. They also destroyed all the Mayan books they could find. With this loss went much of the written wisdom and history of the Maya. Although the Maya were scattered throughout the countryside, they resisted as much as possible Spanish efforts to change their religion and their way of life. In the end, they took some of what the Spanish offered and adapted it to suit their needs.

Meanwhile, the Itzá Maya of Lake Petén Itzá had managed to maintain their traditions by staying out of the wars and remaining hidden in the jungle, to which they had fled in 1460. Eventually, however, the Spaniards found out about them and set out to conquer them, too. In 1697, a large band of soldiers descended on them, and despite fierce resistance from the Itzá Maya, their towns were destroyed and their people killed or dispersed. It was the final victory over the old Mayan city-states.

The Mayan people who survived the years of warfare were often badly treated by the Spanish and the mestizos who ruled after Mexico gained its independence from Spain in 1821. In 1847 and 1860, there were uprisings among the Maya in the Yucatán area; hundreds of thousands of lives were lost. In 1910, there was rebellion in the Quintana Roo area, and again in 1994, in the Chiapas state of Mexico. Their civilization may have been broken, but the Maya remain fierce and independent in spirit today.

Opposite:
Chichén Itzá was once a great Mayan city. Here, the remains of an observatory stand as testament to the advanced culture of this conquered people.

Chapter

5

The Andes and Western South America

After Vasco Nuñéz de Balboa discovered the way across Central America to the Pacific Ocean in 1513, the Spanish began to build ships on the western coast and sail southward from there in search of gold. They heard stories of a people who lived high in the Andes mountains whose cities were filled with magnificent treasures.

These were the people of the great Inca empire, which was made up of some 6 million members of numerous tribes who paid tribute to the Supreme Inca, the king of the dominant tribe. He was said to be a descendant of the first man, and created by the sun. All the people under him became known as the Inca. They spoke a language called Quechua and gave up all independence to the Inca in exchange for his protection.

The great city of Cuzco was the heart of the Inca empire, which stretched for thousands of miles along the Andes to the north, south, and east.

Opposite:
Long before the Spanish conquered Cuzco, the Inca built a fortress outside the city called Sacsayhuamán. This doorway, made of huge boulders, was made without cement or mortar.

Death of the Emperor

A Spanish conquistador named Francisco Pizarro was determined to be the one to conquer this empire. Heading out from Panama in 1524, he got as far as Colombia, and in 1526 he reached Ecuador. In 1527, he entered Peru and was successful enough to be given the title of governor of Peru by the Spanish government.

In that same year, the Incan emperor, Huayna Capac, and thousands of his people, died in a smallpox epidemic brought by the Spaniards to South America. Two of his sons, Huáscar and Atahualpa, were vying for the throne left vacant by their father's death as Pizarro was preparing to

Francisco Pizarro met with Atahualpa before attacking the city of Cajamarca. When Atahualpa refused to convert to Christianity, he was captured and later killed by Pizarro.

invade their kingdom. Atahualpa had more of the experienced warriors on his side, and succeeded in capturing (and later killing) Huáscar. The deaths of many thousands of Inca warriors, however, left the empire vulnerable to the coming Spanish invasion.

In 1532, Pizarro and an army of 200 Spaniards invaded Peru, robbing the villages they passed through of any treasure they could find. In November of that year, the Spanish soldiers reached the city of Cajamarca, high in the Andes. The city itself was deserted, but Atahualpa was camped nearby with his army of 40,000 men. Pizarro lined up his horses, his men, and his cannons in the center of the city, and invited Atahualpa to come to talk with him. When Atahualpa arrived, he was carried on a golden litter and surrounded by thousands of his people.

A priest approached the Inca and told him that he must become a Christian. Atahualpa was insulted. He refused to give up his gods and his religion. Pizarro then gave the order for attack. Atahualpa was captured, and thousands of Inca were killed on the spot.

Atahualpa offered an incredible ransom in return for his freedom. He said that his people would fill one whole room with gold and another with silver if the Spanish would let him go. Many loads of precious objects were carried to Cajamarca in the arms of Inca and on the backs of llamas. Rather than appreciating the exquisite craftsmanship of the jewelry, vessels, and artwork, much of it more beautiful than anything found in Europe, the Spanish promptly melted it down into bars that could be divided among themselves.

After collecting the ransom, Pizarro had Atahualpa strangled, on August 29, 1533. This left the empire in a state of confusion, for the people were completely dependent on their leader. Pizarro moved on to the Inca capital of Cuzco. There he appointed an Inca to rule over the empire—but in name only, because the Inca would actually be governed by Pizarro himself. In 1535, he founded the city of Lima. From there he set out expeditions in all directions, hoping to find more gold.

A New Empire

The Spaniards established a system called *encomienda*, by which soldiers and settlers were given land to mine or farm, as well as any native people who happened to live on that land as slaves. This was similar to the European serf system.

Over the next century, hundreds of thousands of natives died. They died digging in the mines and carrying heavy loads over the mountains. They also died from European diseases, from lack of good food, and from being beaten.

As happened in other areas of the New World, this harsh rule led to periodic revolts by the natives and the mestizos. In 1780, a series of rebellions were led by a mestizo who took the name Túpac Amaru II, claiming to be a descendant of the last Inca ruler. Some 60,000 Inca descendants rose with him to fight. In 1781, Túpac Amaru II was captured and killed, but his brother continued the fight. In 1782, about ninety of Amaru's followers were sent to Spain in chains, and the Inca uprising ended.

Other tribes in the Andes fared no better. In 1536, Gonzalo Jimenez de Quesada ventured up the Magdalena River in Colombia, conquered a tribe called the Muisca, and plundered their cache of gold and emeralds. He founded the Spanish city of Bogotá in the Colombian Andes in 1538.

Another native group of the northern Andes was the Tairona. These people fiercely resisted the Spanish invasion of their lands in the sixteenth century, but were gradually pushed into higher parts of the Sierra Nevada de Santa Marta, where they became known as the Kogi and were left mainly to themselves. The Kogi still live in this region.

Today, members of the Kogi tribe live as their ancestors did. Here, in the village of Marwámaque, thatched houses are their primary dwellings.

To the south of the Inca empire lived other native groups as well. One of these, the Araucanians, also known as the Mapuche, had fought off the armies of the Inca for many years before the Spanish arrived. The Mapuche continued to fight these new invaders even after the Inca were conquered.

In 1535, Francisco Pizarro, now viceroy of Peru, sent his second-in-command, Diego de Almagro, over the Andes into Chile to fight the Mapuche and to look for gold. Many of the Spaniards and the natives they took along as guides and carriers died of starvation, thirst, and exposure even before they encountered the Mapuche, who attacked and killed many more of them. What was left of the Almagro party was forced to return to Peru. Instead of rewarding Almagro for his efforts, Pizarro had him put to death for a made-up charge of treason. Three years later, Almagro's sons murdered Pizarro.

In 1541, a conquistador named Pedro de Valdivia led an expedition into Chile. He decided to march down the coast rather than try to cross the mountains. As he advanced, he killed all the coastal natives he encountered, so that they would not be able to attack him on his return. At one point along the way he stopped, built a great fort that he called Santiago, and gave all the surrounding land to his soldiers. He did not kill the natives here, because his soldiers would need them to work their land.

The natives, however, had other ideas. For nearly 300 years, they had fought the Spanish in what is known as the Wars of Arauco. One of their leaders was a man named Lautaro, who had been a servant of Valdivia in the past. After escaping from the Spaniards, Lautaro became a war chief among his people, and he captured and killed his former master during this expedition.

For a long time, the Spaniards stayed out of southern Chile, leaving it to the native people they were unable to conquer. In the late 1800s, however, the natives of this area were finally forced onto reservations. The Mapuche tried their best to adapt to this new life. Many of them still live in the south of Chile and farm the land that they are proud to call their own.

Opposite:
This monument pays tribute to Lautaro, who led his people to battle against the Spanish during the Wars of Arauco.

Chapter

6

The Amazon Basin and Southeastern South America

The Amazon Basin makes up a very large part of South America. Some areas of it have remained unexplored to this day by anyone other than small bands of native people. Since the beginning of the sixteenth century, the rainforest that surrounds the Amazon River has been the last refuge for many natives seeking to avoid contact with European invaders.

When Europeans first traveled up the dark waters of the Amazon, there were probably about 5 million people living in numerous tribal groups throughout the millions of acres of jungle. Disease, warfare, and the destruction of the rainforest have reduced those numbers to perhaps a few hundred thousand natives.

Opposite:
A young boy paddles his canoe on the Amazon River in Brazil. Before the arrival of European explorers, about 5 million native people lived in the Amazon Basin.

A Portuguese Colony

In 1500, the Portuguese admiral Pedro Alvares Cabral sighted the coast of Brazil when he was supposed to be sailing down the coast of Africa on his way to India. Some people think that he had been blown off course and that his finding Brazil was an accident. Others think that this was part of a plan by Portugal to make sure that Spain did not claim all of the New World and its treasures for itself.

In any case, Cabral sent a party of men ashore, where they were greeted by naked men carrying bows and arrows. These were probably people of the Tupi family of tribes, some of whom had recently migrated to the Atlantic shores of Brazil from farther southwest. There were also tribes of Arawaks, Caribs, Gê-speaking people, and other groups in the Amazon Basin area.

In Brazil, an old Portuguese fort was erected during the European invasion. As Europeans claimed more of the New World for themselves, they established bases from which they could launch expeditions.

❖

49

Like Columbus, Cabral thought the natives would be easy to convert to Christianity because they were so eager to please and so good at imitating the Europeans. They willingly helped the Portuguese load huge brazilwood trees into their ship to send back to Portugal.

Over the next few years, the Portuguese, the Spanish, and the French sent expeditions to explore the Atlantic coast of South America. They traded iron axes and knives with the natives in return for their assistance in cutting down, hauling, and loading wood. Relations between the Europeans and the natives were good until the native people had all the tools they needed and became less willing to help the Europeans. The Europeans then encouraged warfare among the tribes so that they could take the prisoners of war as slaves. When even this did not provide enough slaves to work the sugar plantations that had been established, the Europeans themselves became slave hunters.

The honorable and traditional course for the Tupi and other native groups was to fight in the face of such infringement. They tried to push the invaders back into the sea. The Europeans did not seem to understand that for the natives, becoming a slave was worse than dying—worse, even, than being killed and eaten by enemies. One Tupi warrior who had been enslaved said, "When I reflect that I am the son of one of the great men of my country and that my father was feared and that everyone surrounded him to listen to him, and seeing myself now a slave without paint and with no feathers fastened to my head or on my arms— when I think all this I wish I were dead."

Many of the natives who were not captured retreated farther into the rainforest to escape the European invasion. The Europeans soon began pushing deeper into this territory, the Portuguese from the east coast and the Spaniards from the west.

❖

50

Down the Amazon

In 1539, Gonzalo Pizarro, brother of Francisco Pizarro who conquered the Inca, led an expedition eastward from Peru in the hope of finding gold and spices that were rumored to be found in that direction. As the soldiers made their way through torrential rain, and then through heavy snowstorms high in the Andes, many of the 4,000 natives who had been forced to accompany them died. As Spaniards and natives made their way down the eastern side of the mountains and entered the vast Amazon rainforest, things only got worse. They had to hack their way through the dense vegetation with hatchets, all the while soaked by the unceasing rain. Most of their supplies had been used up or abandoned in the mountains, and they were slowly starving to death. In desperation, they built a boat with which to sail down the river that they had been following. A small group would be sent in the boat to find food and return with it as soon as possible.

The leader of this group was Francisco de Orellana. After a few days, Orellana had not found any food and decided that the current that swept him along was too strong to allow him to return to Pizzaro and the others. He later said that he had had no choice but to continue downriver. Pizarro waited for Orellana to return and then chose to follow the river, hoping with each passing minute to see Orellana returning with food. As his men continued to die of either jungle diseases or starvation, Pizarro realized that their only hope was to return to Peru, as bad as the return journey would be. None of the natives with him survived, and only about one third of the Spaniards lived.

In the meantime, Orellana, who had continued to ride what was the River Napo, was starving as well. Suddenly, he saw a native village on the shores of the river, the first the Spaniards had seen in a long time. Finding it deserted, they

devoured all the food they could find. When the native people returned to the village, Orellana managed to persuade them to keep feeding the Spaniards while they built a better boat. They then proceeded down the river. As they traveled, they encountered, and fought with, many more groups of natives, most of whom had never seen Europeans. It is said that one of the groups Orellana's party met was a band of warrior women called Amazons, whose name was given to the great river that Orellana followed all the way to the Atlantic Ocean. He had succeeded in crossing the continent of South America at its widest point, a journey that was thousands of miles long. To this day, few people have traveled the full length of the Amazon River as Orellana did.

Soldiers, Missionaries, and Bandeirantes

At about the same time that Pizarro and Orellana were fending off starvation along the Amazon, other Spaniards were exploring and colonizing the southern part of Brazil and what is now Paraguay, Uruguay, and Argentina. The city of Asunción was founded in 1537 among the Guaraní. These people were friendly toward the Spanish, joining them as allies, and allowing the Spaniards to marry their women. When the Spaniards treated them as slaves, however, there were revolts, which led to a decline in the native population as the Spanish and mestizo population grew.

In 1541, Cabeza de Vaca, who had survived a long trek across northern Mexico, traveled south over land to Asunción, in central South America. He was one of the few explorers to treat the natives well. He insisted that his men buy food from the Guaraní with trade goods rather than just taking it, as many other soldiers and explorers did.

Besides soldiers and colonists, many Catholic missionaries also came to Brazil. Most of them were good men who believed that establishing missions where the natives could be put to work while being taught the Christian religion was the right thing to do. Here the natives could be protected somewhat from slave hunters. All too often, though, the natives of the missions died by the thousands from diseases that they caught from the Europeans.

Moreover, the missionaries were not always able to save the natives from the slave hunters, especially when large groups of *bandeirantes* attacked. These bands of "pioneers," usually of mixed European and native parentage, began to spread throughout this territory during the late seventeenth and early eighteenth centuries. Sometimes they were in search of gold or land on which to settle. Often their quest was for slaves, and the natives of the missions were all-too-easy targets.

Using an ancient method, a Peruvian tree is tapped for rubber. Thousands of natives were enslaved to collect and process rubber during the 1800s.

In the 1800s, it was the "rubber boom" that most threatened the native population. Thousands of natives were enslaved and forced to work in the gathering and smoking of rubber. Some wealthy rubber barons even maintained private armies, to keep their slaves under control.

After the rubber boom, vast areas of the rainforest were cleared to make room for plantations. Large tracts of land were sold to rich buyers in Brazil, the United States, and Europe. The natives were simply "cleared" from the land, one way or another.

Slowly, Brazil and the other nations of eastern South America gained their independence from Europe and

Xingu National Park

In 1961, the Brazilian government's National Foundation for Assistance to Indians created Xingu National Park. This national park is quite different from the ones found in the United States. It is not a place for tourists to spend a vacation surrounded by beautiful scenery; it is, instead, a piece of land reserved for use by some of the native people of Brazil.

Xingu National Park was created in large part due to the efforts of three brothers, Orlando, Claudio, and Leonardo Villas Boas. In the 1940s, these brothers participated in a program known as "Brazil's March to the West." This was a program intended to open up land in the Amazon rainforest to colonization. But after exploring the land, the Villas Boas brothers discovered that the rainforest

in general, and the Xingu River region in particular, was already richly inhabited by a variety of plants, animals, and people. The people were members of numerous different native tribes. They spoke many different languages, including all four of the main linguistic groups of northeastern South America (Tupi, Gê, Arawak, and Carib). These tribal peoples lived much as their ancestors had when Europeans first came to the shores of Brazil in 1500, and even as those natives' ancestors had lived for centuries before that.

The Villas Boas brothers realized that development of the Amazon rainforest would totally disrupt, and perhaps destroy, the lives of natives who lived there. The brothers decided that at least part of the answer was for the government to create a place

became more modern. Many of the native peoples were either assimilated or ignored. Many traces of their cultures, however, are found even in these modern times. For example, most of the people of Paraguay today speak both Spanish and Guaraní.

where the Amazon peoples could live according to their traditions, removed and undisturbed by modern society.

The brothers selected an area along the Xingu where some tribes were already living. They arranged for members of about a dozen other tribes to move there, too, even tribes that were considered warlike. The brothers knew that if warlike tribes were not protected, they would be killed by settlers who felt threatened by them.

Today, all of these tribes live in separate villages within Xingu. Each tribe retains characteristics that set it apart from its neighbors, but they all also have much in common. The tribes have a limited amount of contact with the outside world. Many of these people, however, have been vaccinated to protect them against the deadly diseases that killed so many natives of the Americas.

Leonardo Villas Boas died in 1961, but Orlando and Claudio continued to fight on behalf of the tribes of the Amazon. For many years, they tried to keep outsiders from interfering with life within the park as much as possible. Sometimes they failed, as in the 1980s, when a highway was built through a portion of the park.

It remains to be seen whether this attempt at preserving the culture of the native tribes will succeed in the long run. Repeatedly, the modern world closes in and invades the borders of Xingu, and threatens the way of life of its inhabitants. The Villas Boas brothers, however, and others who help them, remain dedicated to the principle of protecting the natives. As the brothers have said, "The true defense of the Indian is to respect him and to guarantee his existence according to his own values."

The Kaipo is a Brazilian tribe that has kept many of its traditional ways. Here, three Kaipo children pose for a photo.

Native Cultures in a Modern World

More than 500 years have passed since Christopher Columbus made his historic landing. Explorers of the New World often remarked on how numerous the natives were, how long they lived, and how healthy they seemed. After the invasion of Europeans that followed, this changed. Millions of native people died as the result of warfare, slavery, and disease. In some cases, entire groups of people and their cultures were wiped out. In other cases, whole groups were largely assimilated into the mainstream of society and intermarried with the Europeans. Many of the people of Central and South America can trace their ancestry to both European invaders and native people.

In yet other cases, native people took some of what the Europeans had to offer and adapted it to blend with their traditions. Although most of these somewhat modified native cultures remain independent, they tend to be very poor and to live apart from the mainstream of modern life in their homelands.

Finally, there are some places where the native cultures have managed to remain virtually unchanged in all this time. This is seen most dramatically in the Amazon Basin, where groups like the Yanomami of Venezuela and Brazil and the Waorani of Equador are very similar to the people who greeted Columbus, Cabral, de Orellana, and the others. The history of their contact with the people now "invading" the rainforest is being written today.

Glossary

aqueduct A pipe, or canal, used for transporting water.

archaeologist A scientist who studies ancient civilizations—
the histories and cultures of the past.

assimilated Having been made similar to those around
one, as when the native people became more like the
Spanish.

bandeirante A "pioneer" of Brazil who traveled beyond
the settled frontier in search of gold, land, and slaves.

bubonic plague A highly contagious and usually fatal
disease.

cacique A leader or chief of certain Caribbean, Mexican,
and Central and South American native groups.

cannibalism The eating of human beings by human beings.

causeway A bridge built over water with sections that can
be raised or removed.

colonist A person who moves to a new place to establish a
settlement, or colony.

conquistador A conqueror, particularly a soldier or an
explorer from Spain.

encomienda A system by which the Spanish colonists were granted control of land and of the native people who lived on it.

epidemic An outbreak of a disease that spreads rapidly to many people.

mestizo A person with both European and Indian parents or ancestors.

nomad A person who moves his or her home from place to place in search of food.

plantation A large farm, usually specializing in the growing of one particular crop, and often worked by people who live on the grounds of the plantation.

pre-Columbian A term referring to events in the Americas before 1492, the year of the arrival of Christopher Columbus in the New World and the beginning of the European invasion.

pueblo A type of home built of stone or clay by certain native peoples of the American Southwest, having many levels.

rubber barons Persons who gained great wealth and power in the rubber industry during the rubber boom.

tribute A payment, or tax, given to a ruler.

Chronology

1492	Christopher Columbus lands on San Salvador, builds a fort called Navidad on Hispaniola, and initiates the European invasion of the Americas.
1498	On his third voyage, Columbus lands briefly on the northwest coast of South America.
1500	Pedro Alvares Cabral lands on the coast of Brazil.
1502	First contact between the Maya and the Europeans occurs when Columbus encounters a group of Maya during his fourth voyage.
1513	Vasco Núñez de Balboa crosses the Isthmus of Panama to the Pacific Ocean.
1519	Hernando Cortés begins his march into Mexico.
1521	Tenochtitlán is destroyed and the Aztec empire falls to Cortés.
1527	The Spanish begin attacking the Maya in Yucatán and Guatemala.
1532	Francisco Pizarro invades Peru and captures Atahualpa, the Inca emperor, whom he later kills.
1536	Alvar Núñez Cabeza de Vaca walks across Texas and northern Mexico.
1537	The city of Asunción is founded among the Guaraní in central South America.
1539	Gonzalo Pizarro leads an expedition over the Andes from Peru. Francisco de Orellana breaks off from this group and follows the Amazon to the Atlantic Ocean.

1540   Francisco Vásquez de Coronado leads an expedition from Mexico City into northwestern Mexico and the American southwest.

1541   Pedro de Valdivia leads an expedition into Chile and establishes a fort at Santiago.

1697   The Maya of Lake Petén Itzá are defeated.

1780   Túpac Amaru II leads an uprising of Inca.

1800s The rubber boom in the Amazon Basin leads to the enslavement of hundreds of natives.

1847- Maya uprisings in southern Mexico and the
1860   Yucatán result in the loss of hundreds of thousands of lives.

❖

61

Further Reading

Fritz, Jean. *Where Do You Think You're Going, Christopher Columbus?* New York: G.P. Putnam's Sons, 1980.

Hintz, Martin. *Chile.* Chicago: Childrens Press, 1985.

Jacobs, Francine. *The Tainos, The People Who Welcomed Columbus.* New York: G.P. Putnam's Sons, 1992.

Lepthien, Emilie U. *Peru.* Chicago: Childrens Press, 1992.

McCall, Barbara. *Native American Culture: The European Invasion.* Vero Beach, FL: Rourke Publications, 1994.

Morrison, Marion. *Indians of the Amazon.* Vero Beach, FL: Rourke Publications, 1989.

_____. *Colombia.* Chicago: Childrens Press, 1990.

Sherrow, Victoria. *Native Latin American Cultures: Daily Customs.* Vero Beach, FL: Rourke Publications, Inc., 1995.

Stein, R. Conrad. *Francisco de Coronado.* Chicago: Childrens Press, 1992.

_____. *Mexico.* Chicago: Childrens Press, 1984.

Vásquez, Ana María B. *Panama.* Chicago: Childrens Press, 1991.

Index

Photo Credits

Cover and pages 6, 22, 24, 33: ©Robert Frerck/Odyssey Productions/Chicago; pp. 10, 12, 16, 26, 29, 34, 40, 51: ©North Wind Picture Archives; pp. 11, 15, 27, 38, 43, 44, 48: ©Chip and Rosa Maria de la Cueva Peterson; p. 19: Odyssey Productions/ Chicago; p. 20: ©Thom Buchanan/Haller/Buchanan Studio; p. 30: ©Robert B. Pickering; p. 36: Mexican Government Tourism Office; p. 46: ©Craig Duncan/DDB Stock Photo; p. 53: ©Bates Littlehales/Earth Scenes; p. 56: ©Nair Benedicto/DDB Stock Photo.